Monday

It was a wet day.

Tuesday

It was a windy day.

I went to the shops.

Wednesday

It was a sunny day.

I went to the pool.

Thursday

It was a hot day.

I went to the park.

It was a fun day.

Look at me, Mum.

Look at me, Mum.

Look at me on my bike.

Look at me, Mum.

Look at me on my bike.

Look at me, Mum.

Oh, no!

Look at me!

Go away, Floppy.

Go away, Floppy.

We are skipping.

Go away, Floppy.

We are painting.

Come back, Floppy.

Floppy, come back.

We are sorry.

Come and look at this.

Come and look at this.

Is it a big monster?

Come and look at this.

Is it a big dinosaur?

Come and look at this.

Is it a big giant?

No. It is Dad.

We are all in red.

We are all in blue.

3

Come on the reds!

Come on the blues!

Who is in red?

Who is in blue?

We are all muddy.

Can you see us?

Can you see me?

Yes, I can see you.

Can you see me?

Yes, we can see you.

Can you see me?

Yes, we can see you.

We can all see Dad.